Shh!
SIDEPIECE
be quiet

POETIC WOMAN

Copyright © 2021 Victoria Kirby
All rights reserved. No part of this publication may be reproduced, distributed, or transmitted in any form or by any means, including photocopying, recording, or other electronic or mechanical methods, without the prior written permission of the publisher, except in the case of brief quotations embodied in critical reviews and certain other noncommercial uses permitted by copyright law. For permission requests, write to the publisher, addressed "Attention: Book Rights and Permission," at the address below.
Published in the United States of America
ISBN 978-1-955243-13-1 (SC)

Victoria Kirby
222 West 6th Street
Suite 400, San Pedro, CA, 90731
www.stellarliterary.com
Order Information and Rights Permission:

Quantity sales. Special discounts might be available on quantity purchases by corporations, associations, and others. For details, contact the publisher at the address above.
For Book Rights Adaptation and other Rights Permission. Call us at toll-free 1-888-945-8513 or send us an email at admin@stellarliterary.com.

CONTENTS

Preface 1

Dedication 3

Chapter 1. The Sex Walk 5

Chapter 2. Thirsty Baby Daddy 11

Letters From Hurt, Pain & Observation............................... 21

Infidelity Receipts 35

Inspirations In My Life... 43

About the Author 45

PREFACE

It's something about how most older men will have a younger woman reaching her highest peak of climax when he first begins to make passionate love to her. That feeling of when it's all over then she has that weak knees feeling wanting to go back for another round. Just as in to remember do they shower together to begin round two. Cause there's nothing like having some hot steamy passionate sex in the shower with the one you love. Or do they part separate ways knowing that they both might be dating someone else. Because some people relationships are complicated to them. While other people are happy in their relationship or marriage. Though we know it's not a such thing as the perfect marriage or relationship to begin with. Though whenever someone wants something or someone they have to work hard to get them. And extra harder to keep them. It's just that some people value the person that they're with and other people might be waiting for you to make one too many slip ups.

DEDICATION

This book is dedicated to every woman who knows her worth and when to leave a relationship or marriage when it's too toxic.

CHAPTER 1

The Sex Walk

Intimate infatuation and the development of deep feelings go hand and hand when it comes to satisfying a woman's needs. Sure every man has needs as well as a woman does. Though, maybe it's just something about how a woman breasts smother a man face that makes her so attracted to him. Or maybe it's something else. Some women are known for their reputations especially in the streets.

Truth be told, it could be the conversation a woman gives to a man that makes him want her more. Every relationship, friendship and marriage comes with breath taking moments. Being a younger woman myself with the experience of being in a relationship with an older man for eleven years had its breath taking moments. He was every bit of a gentleman. And now a days a good gentleman is hard to find.

Not only did I love all 5 foot 9 inches of him. But, when it came to the bedroom loving man it was on point. I've had regular sex in my past two relationships before dating an older man. But, once I had met my soul-mate in my third relationship it was different. Different how some of you may ask yourself? The man I loved knew how to make love to me like no one else had ever done. He was an experienced older man. When we first made love the after feeling left me weak at the knees. I recall him asking what was wrong with me. I said you got me feeling like this. Then he said to me haven't you felt that way before.

Now, if you really think about it once a man samples a woman goods he wants more. And when he realizes you with a different walk he knows his job has been done. Whether it's the first time a woman has had a single orgasm or she's a pro every man has his preference.

Just like in an instant split second when a man realizes that a woman's whole mind frame is different. He thinks to himself has aunt flo visited her this month? Is she frustrated from her job? Is she pregnant? Has menopause kicked in early? Or is she simply not in the mood tonight? Rests assure it could be a combination of any of the five. Just give her a little breathing space.

She'll come around eventually. The moment you rub her the wrong way is when she'll be turned off by you. If she's loyal to you she'll know what she has at home. What seems to be difficult for some men and women to understand is that loyalty is hard to come by. You think that just because you've known a person for so long that they're going to be loyal to you.

Think again, giving a woman good sex whenever she wants can still make her have some second thoughts. She might not be happy in other areas of your relationship. But, you say to yourself at least my D-game is on point. You might think it's on point and could be wrong about that too. That might've been something she was just telling you not to hurt your feelings at the time you were inside of her.

Both older and younger men fail to realize you can't physically or mentally abuse a woman at all and think that you're going to get away with it. Don't expect things to be okay by trying to do her makeup for her if she wears makeup. Or by buying her a pair of dark shades to cover that black eye you just gave her. Some women have themselves believing oh it was an accident. That he love you and won't do it again. And that you shouldn't have said something that made him that upset to just up and hit you or threaten your life.

Nevertheless some women look for men with the total package. A man who treats her like a queen and doesn't abuse her. A man who has just enough experience to teach her new things. A man who's going to love all her curves. Someone who will sacrifice time with his boys just to be with you. And tells his boys that he'll have to take a rain check on the game later for them to record it or something.

In reality some men and women take quality time for granted. Try to spend every moment you can with the ones that you say that you love. Remember to always protect yourself first. Love yourself if no one else will love you. Self-love is such an important factor in life. Without self-love how will you know how to love someone that you say that you love or have deep feelings for.

Just like in an instant moment when some men and women thinks it's okay to hit it raw. Raw or no raw there's always Encare that can be used in place of a condom. Encare should be used 5-10 minutes before intimacy. Sure enough Encare has a woman feeling all warm on the inside. But, I'd rather have a warm feeling any day of the week verses catching an STD. Trying to get rid of an STD or catching one is something most women have never had to worry about. I for one can say that I have never had to worry about having any type of diseases to worry about catching at all.

Being cautious and alert is the best ways to be even if some people are afraid to go get tested. It's better to be tested and know your status. Then to not know at all and be even more stressed about your situation. Because in most cases a woman might either commit suicide or think about committing it. Never make it seem easy for a man to talk you out of your panties. Then again what you won't do for him he might find someone that will. Being that of why some women have such high standards.

Just as in when a man voices his opinion on a group of teen's sex conversation of oral sex. He said that all they probably do is hold the D. That a woman 25 and older wouldn't hold the D because they would know what they're doing. Then he mentioned that he wouldn't date a woman that couldn't make scratch cornbread.

He also mentions that he dates baby mamas and aunties. With the fact of saying that he likes to perform. He wants a woman that can hang. Because soon as he gets two shots of gin in his neck he'll beat his meat if he has to. Needless to say that was more information then I wanted to hear him say to begin with. But, sometimes grown folks conversations can get quite overwhelming for some people. They would rather you change the subject and talk about something else.

Needless to say, he thinks that no single woman should be writing love novels. Not knowing whether or not if that single woman just doesn't want to be loved anymore. That she loves going home to a cold bed at night. Not seeing that at least she doesn't have to worry about any drama. About who's beefing over a piece of beefcake?

Personally speaking, I get my share of drama from work conversations and the customers. Some drunken sobbing customers try to get off the most steam. They tend to forget what they said the next day. Some of them might or might not apologize to you. But as a worker having to service the public it's just certain things that you will or won't take from a customer. In some instances the customers isn't always right.

For instance, if you can't relate to a certain conversation of discussion then you might be lame to others. But, I'd rather be a lame when it comes to having a sex conversation with an 18 year old. First thing they might fix their mouth to say is man I know I shouldn't have told you that about my sex life to begin with. True enough I was once 18 years old myself. It's just that certain 18 year olds are either more experienced then you. Or they just want to know would you let a dude hit it and pull out raw.

No matter or not if a dude says this is me you know I love you. Some women find themselves doing a smell test on their man. Just because I've heard of what the smell test is doesn't means that I've ever had to do one on anyone that I've ever dated. It's just that I wasn't having that I was the only woman that they were dating when we were dating each other.

For those that don't know, some women will ask her man to pull down his boxers and she'll smell his D. Soon as she discovers the sex smell on him, he's in the doghouse for sure. To make matters worse he better hope she doesn't have a black light. A black light that'll detect any nut stains on his clothes or jewelry. She'll then find a brick to bust his car windows. Some special key to key up his car. Or a gun to shoot him for cheating on her. All in a matter of minutes. Sex can make a man or woman do some crazy things.

What's really crazy, awkward, and scary is when a man tells you the longest he's ever had sex. Really though, you would think only some women have that conversation with other women. Nevertheless, I've never had the conversation with another female acquaintance. That's when it would be time to change the conversation. Those types of conversations are conversations you should have with your man or lover only.

Ain't that much because she's my best friend in the world at all. A woman who's another woman best friend won't tell you what color her panties is, so why tell you so much details about her sex life. Then again you have some women that will go so far as to tell you how long their man D is. Best believe ain't that much love for a best friend in the world to be knowing what goes on behind the doors of your bedroom.

Believe it or not some women think that they know when a woman hasn't had any D in a while. First sign would be the way a woman acts around a group of people. Another sign would be if she ignores your phone calls or text messages. She might tell you girl I'm going to hit you up later I'm busy right now.

My opinion is that, some people look at sex as an extra curriculum activity. Something to do just to pass time. Not always the fact of loving and trying to please someone you say that you have deep feelings for. For example, if you hurt a man or a woman's feelings you might be headed to losing the best friend that you've ever had. And we all know that good friends and good mates are both hard to come by.

CHAPTER 2

Thirsty Baby Daddy

A in't any way that a man who says that he has a good woman at home should be sliding into his baby mama DM. But, the second his main chic accuses him of another woman is when some men think it's time to go search for happiness elsewhere. First thing he might say to himself is, man I'm tired of you accusing me of cheating all the time listening to your friend girls all up in your ear.

Just soon as a man finds himself in the single lane, not a single soul wants to look his way. Soon as a woman block you from one social media site don't means that gives you the right to follow her on another one. In all actuality she blocked you for a reason. She doesn't want to be your friend. Her only concern is the child that the two of you share in common. Though the moment you let that child down is when she might lose all respect for you. Think about it then you have no one to blame but yourself for your own actions of breaking promises that you made to your son or daughter.

Being that with some baby daddies try to stay their distance when their baby mama is either dating someone else or married to them. In his mind, he figures I'm going to respect her boundaries. Then again, he might think soon as she needs a shoulder to lean on that he's going to be there for her no matter what hands down.

Believe it or not, no woman or man should want to be each other's part time lover. In the long run someone is going to end up with a broken heart. Remember a man that shows respect will get respect from his baby mama. Trust that the moment when your child sees you lay a hand on his or her mama the wrong way its curtains for you. You might as well prepare yourself to have some bond money saved up. And think of the only person you're going to use as your one phone call.

In my opinion, no man should want to serve time over a child support bench warrant. Then again, you have some men that don't care now a days. Because the minute they conceive their tenth child is the moment they don't have to pay child support. They might tell their baby mama I'm not giving you a dime of my money.

Just as in another instant, some women use child support to get their toes and hair done. While on the other had other women will use child support to go get the necessary items that their child needs. No matter what the case might be a boy needs his father in his life. Some women can't teach a boy how to be a man. On the other hand you have some women that have to play both roles in their child's life.

Without a father or a father figure in a boy's life there's no telling what might happen. But again there are some women who can teach a boy how to be a man. They'll start off with the birds and the bees' conversation. In between those two conversations is education being important and a must in order to be whatever they want to be when they grow up. Last but certainly not least is for a child to choose their friends wisely.

That everyone you think is your friend actually isn't. How you should be able to lay a few dollars on your table and come back to it. Or leave your woman around your friends just to go to the bathroom and come back to her without them being all touchy feely with each other. Just depends on whether your home boys know not to break the bro code whether it's in your face or behind your back.

For example, if your co-worker walks up to you and shows you a message that your baby daddy DM her what would you do? Would you call him thirsty and laugh it off knowing that he suppose to be dating someone else? Or would you tell her to go for it and see how he treats her? In other terms there are ways to tell if you have a thirsty or jealous baby daddy.

1. He slides into your DM following you after you blocked him on another social media site.
2. He'll write you a secret note and say it's from your secret boo.
3. He'll ask whose calling your phone even though ya'll is not even together.
4. He might pay someone to stalk you.
5. He would try to get a job where you work at.
6. He might expose a nude picture of you to the press.
7. He'll try to hook up with your ex best friend to see if it'll make you jealous.
8. He'll tell you who you can and can't be friends with.
9. He might try to mail himself to you via federal express.
10. He'll offer to take you on a weekend getaway to catch up on old times.

No matter the circumstance no man or woman should have to beg for anything. Begging and pleading in some instances makes someone feel less of a man or woman. That's why sometimes it's better for men and women to have their space. Allow just enough space for room for improvement. Without a doubt no woman will always like a man that can't pay his own way at times. Though when a woman pays her own way all the time she might be too boogie in a man's eye.

In my personal opinion, for all the baby mama's who share the same baby daddy they should give their kids a chance to know each other. Let them decide for themselves on whether they want a relationship with their sibling. Truth of the matter is when a child or adult distances themselves from family it's for a reason. Though by, allowing that child to make certain mistakes on their own is how they'll learn.

Realistically speaking, I wished that I would've made better choices when it came to my 2nd baby daddy. I wished that I could've stopped him from getting high and drinking when he did. I should've gone with my first thought and kept our son hidden from him. What really upset me the most is when he denied our son even before he was born. Personally when it all boils down to it, I wished the 3rd relationship I had with my bae that he could've been my 2nd baby daddy.

Sure, some women have regrets from lying down with certain men. Let it also be known that, some men make great fathers and mentors. I would never discredit any man who steps up to the plate to mentor another man's child. Thing of it is, my father and I don't have that bond that most women have with their father. On holidays he doesn't even call just to see how I'm doing. Even on regular days it's the same. And now the cycle continues on with my two sons.

In all actuality, if someone were to ask me what I've learned out of all 3 relationships I've had there's really not much comparison at all. I've learned more with the third relationship I've had than with the first two I had in the past. Maybe because my third relationship lasted the longest. My third relationship lasted 11 years 3 months and 3 weeks. I grew more as a woman and was with a man who loved me no matter what. He never felt like I was smothering him at all.

When it's all said and done if I had a choice, I'd rather someone bring back by bae to life. Without a doubt, no matter how many people think that I'm bitter, I'm really not. In other terms the death of a loved one can make all difference in how some people think and react in everyday life after that. Deep down within, I'm a really cool person to hang around. It's just that all I ask is to not bring any drama types of situations my way. Male or female approach me with a level headed mind.

Remember, silent meditation can make your thoughts and ideas appear clearer to you then you think. And that by listening to music it can relieve some stress from your mind. Just think you might feel much better after listening to some of your favorite music. Not even that you should try keeping a journal of how you feel everyday and compare the days with each other. Know that life is too short to be chasing behind any man or woman. With some people your life depends on your happiness. And happiness starts from within your inner self.

Both men and women should never allow anyone to control where you go and what time you have to be back in the house. We all have only one life to live and we should make the best of it while we can. Because if you have to live your life in fear and with too many regrets then you're not living your life to the fullest. For example here are a few examples of what you should do to live your life to the fullest.

1. If a man or woman feels the need to raise their hand up to in an abusive way then that person isn't for you to be with.
2. If a man or woman feels like it's an issue for you to use their phone then know that person can't be trusted.
3. If your man or woman never takes you out in public and just stays home all the time then that's an issue.
4. If your man or woman is always in your ear about who you have to not be friends with then it's time to go.
5. If your man or woman doesn't complement you occasionally or even everyday then it's time to bounce.
6. If your man or woman calls to tell you that they're going to be working late hours for the day then trust your gut and believe them

7. If you have to distance yourself from family and friends because they have some information that your man or woman might be cheating on you then do just that.
8. If your man or woman feels like it's a woman job to do the dirty laundry all the time then it's time to go.
9. If your man or woman feels like it's a woman job to do the dishes all the time then it's time to go.
10. If your man or woman feel like they can't take out the garbage then it's time to bounce

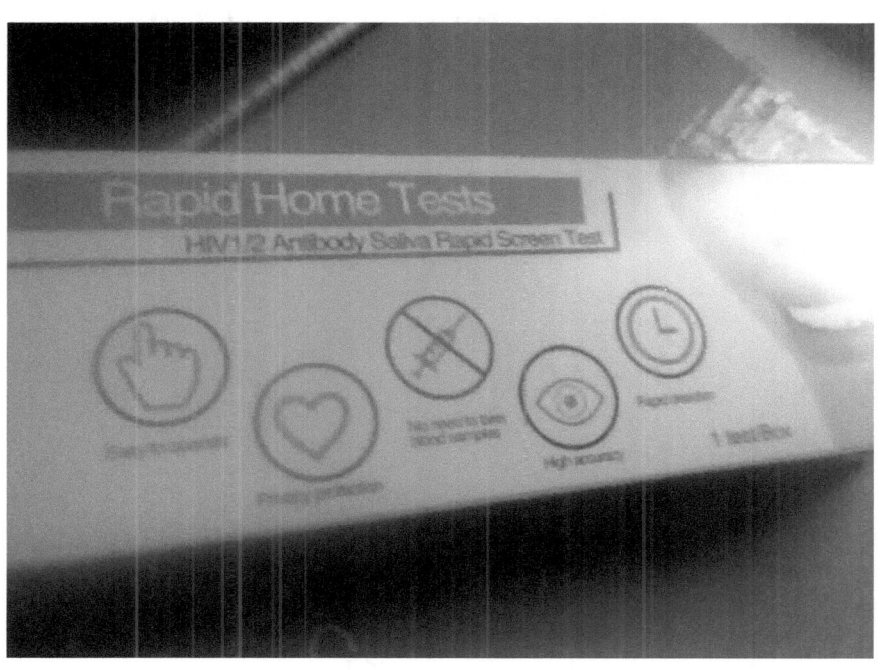

Know your status and inform your mate because it's against the law not to tell your mate if you're HIV positive

Wrap it up and protect yourself don't force yourself
on someone it's called rape and I would think
that you wouldn't want to do time for it.

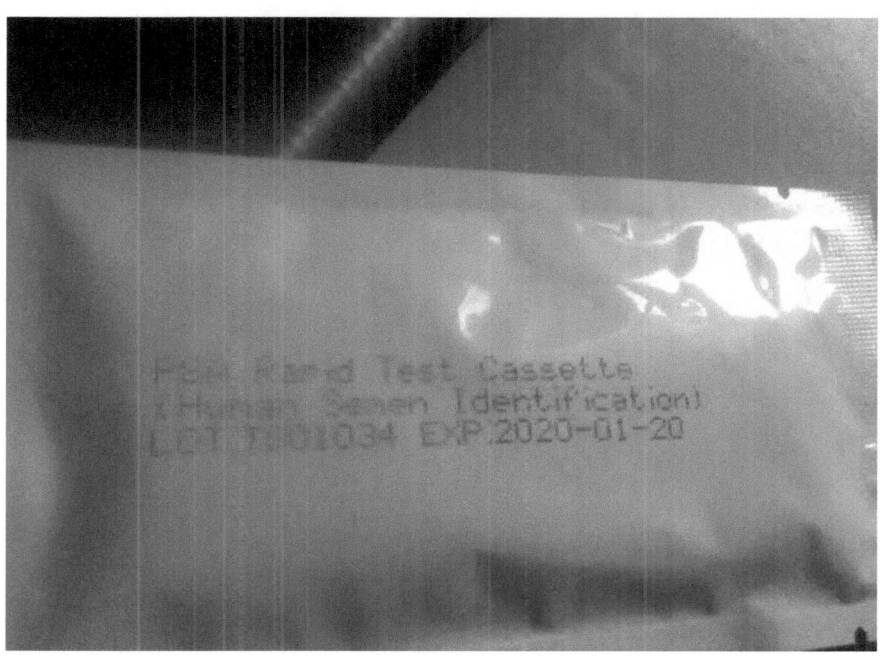

Know that if your mate cheats on you a black light isn't their only option to use.

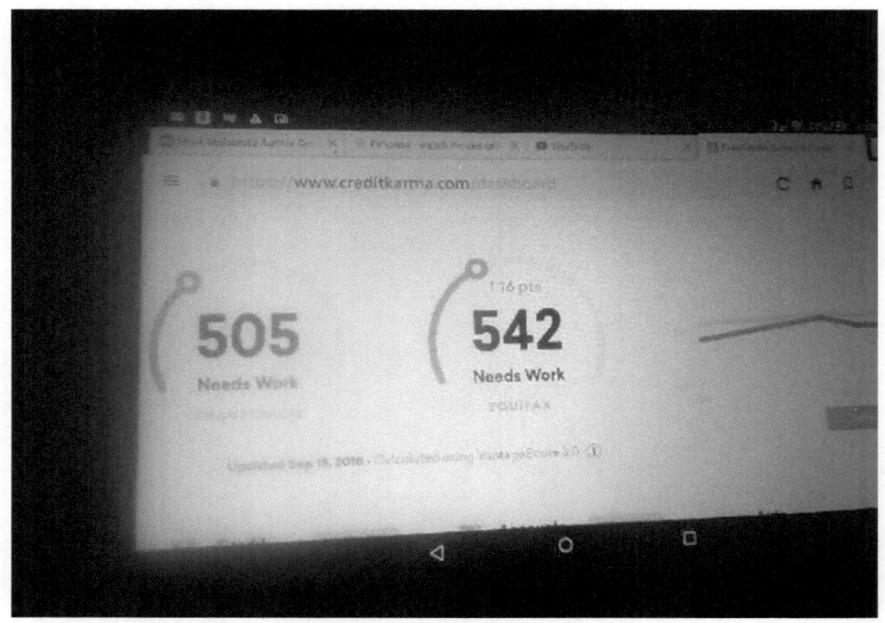

Working on improving my credit score

LETTERS FROM HURT, PAIN & OBSERVATION

SINGLE PARENTS APPRECIATION:

Being that, it's not every day that a single parent is appreciated for all that they do I can relate. As a single parent, we have to work twice as hard as a two parent household. We have to make sure that our kids have clothes, shoes, food and school supplies. Not only that but if we have boys we have to make sure that they get a haircut every week or every other week. Then if it's a girl that we have when she's old enough to get a perm we have to make sure that her hair is straight. And not only that, but we have to make sure that she has sanitary napkins.

WORD TO THE WISE:

Ladies don't ever be afraid to let your man know what your favorite position is. Man get a calendar and keep track of your woman's menstrual cycle so you know when it's time to get you some of that good nookie. Know that it's very likely that a man would want to have sex while a woman is on. And if a woman's kitty cat is dry most men know how to get it wet. While some women would rather play with their battery operated boyfriend and work their way up. Some women can handle a long pipe while others say it hurts and that they're not having sex again after that encounter.

Meanwhile usually when a man or woman says that they'd rather be friends with benefits there seems to be a catch somewhere. They might tell you no strings attached when usually there's a few attached. String one might be you only have sex on their time. Another string might be that he or she doesn't go out with you in public. And a final string might be to co-sign something because you have a better credit score.

TO ALL SIDE PIECES:

Though it may never seem like you ever have a dull moment in your relationship or fling you have going on remember these few things. That man or woman is going home to sleep next to someone else tonight. Surprising him or her with gifts at their job isn't always the thing to do. And last of all remember if your number is saved in his or her phone as home girl or fam then it's best to keep your distance.

FACING REALITY:

Within the four walls of facing reality even the ones you say are your friend will betray your trust. Then, the moment you say very few words to them they wonder what is wrong with you. All the ha ha giggle moments just fly out the window. Rebuilding your friendship to what it used to be might be the last thing to cross your mind. But, what some people might do is know how to be cordial around their so called enemy. Just know to keep your guards up so you won't be blindsided ever again.

SEX RULES 101:

Sex limitations are usually included in some relationships, marriages, or late night booty calls. Just being aware of at least 5 warning signs will keep you alert.

1. All phones, tablets, and t.v.'s must be silenced or powered off
2. Listen closely to see if your mate calls you someone else name
3. Pick some good music to get you in the mood.
4. Remember to put your clothes on the right way after you have finished having sex for those that do quickies.
5. Know that it's okay to be a squirtter if your female and your man is deep inside of you

FEMALE AND MALE INVESTMENTS:

It's simply unfair to the fact that a male or female should have to play the 3rd or 4th wheel in any relationship. When in your mind you think that you have that person all to yourself. Then after finding out from your friends otherwise that your man has a wife and another girlfriend outside of you that you know nothing about. You begin to feel played after asking your man already if he was married and he told you that he was divorced. After the fact you and your girls go to your man house only to be called an investment by him. Then, to hear him introduce his wife and his other girlfriend must've really made you feel low. There's no way no woman who has had not much luck with any relationships in her past should have to go through such a thing. Any man who says he loves his woman whole-heartedly shouldn't make her feel less than of a woman. The same goes for a woman.

GROWN MAN CRY:

Sure some women think something is wrong with a man if she sees him crying. But, let me be the first to say otherwise. I use to date a grown man whom I loved for 11 years before he passed away. I saw him cry a few times. In September of 2016 along-side his hospital bed is the first time that I saw him cry. He found out that he had cancer then. We cried together that day while I was holding his hands. Then another year goes by its September 2017 we cry together once more. This time we found out that he didn't have long to live. Boy how time flies because the last time he cried was two days before he passed away. And besides men cry and hurt just like us women do. We are humans with feelings.

THE HOMIE LANE:

Sometimes in life the homie is just a homie. A male can have a female as his bestie. And vice versa for a female. But, every once in a while a homie might try to cross the friendship border line. Just keep reminding them that you look at them as a brother, sister cousin or uncle. Eventually they might catch the hint. No matter how many times they flirt or offer to buy you something expensive don't make it easy to break the ice.

RELATIONSHIP DEAL BREAKERS:

Within almost every relationship or marriage are quite a few if not more roadblocks that couples go through together.

1. The male or female is too aggressive.
2. The male or female messed up your credit score.
3. You're not financially where you want to be in life.
4. Your relationship is based on sex alone.
5. You spend too much time with the homies.
6. You spend too much time at work.
7. You have nothing in common.
8. You sometimes think about taking two steps backwards.
9. You've never met his or her family.
10. He or she doesn't support your dreams or aspirations.

LIVING BY SELF-LOVE:

Sometimes in life some people become confused the thing called love. Straight, gay, lesbian or bi-sexual everyone deserves to be loved. Some people might say because a person is who they are you don't want to be their friend. Think about it really everyone deserves a few chances to mess up. After those few chances goes by, you then decide is it time to really move on? More importantly love yourself before saying I love you to someone else.

SINGLE BABY MAMA'S:

Single baby mama's including myself knows that some of these baby daddies aren't checking for us. They could care less of what we're doing as the baby mama of their child or kids. Some of us baby mama's could care less of who our baby daddies are sleeping with. Just know that soon as an emergency happens to our kids and the baby daddy isn't informed about it he might get mad. As women we might get called every name in the book under the sun. But, what most baby daddies don't understand is that you shouldn't disrespect your baby mama even if she accidentally gives you a reason to do so.

WHAT MEN WANT:

Fellas hear this loud and clear. No woman wants a man that's going to brag about the size of his penis. Not even that but brag about how long he can go in the bedroom. But, most women do want a man that will love and provide for her. To protect her from any and all possible harm. To be her chief in the kitchen. And not to flirt with her best friend if ya'll break up.

WHAT WOMEN WANT:

Ladies hear me loud and clear. Not many men want a woman that won't work. Unless you have that kind of man that doesn't want his wife or girlfriend to work. It's just that some women like for a man to take charge. And then there are some women who prefer to be independent. You have some of us women that just want to be held. And others who just want to have sex all day. But, when it all boils down to it some women still love for their man or sex buddy to give them a hickie.

LIVING BY THE CODE:

Whether it's the bro code or sister code no one should date someone's former mate if they're your friend. It's against all odds for a male or female to date her ex's best friend. And vice versa for a male. Though an ex is an ex for a reason. To some females and males if your ex isn't with you to you they don't deserve to be happy. Even if it's in your best friend arms that they find their happiness.

FAKING ORGASIMS:

Ladies and fellas hear this loud and clear some of us can tell when the other is faking an orgasm. Some men as well as women have a good ear to detect a fake orgasm. Some women feel after working up a sweat they'll tell you it was okay sex. Then you have some men that'll say they were knee deep into the kitty cat. So either it's the man or woman who needs to put their all into it.

NOTHING HURTS:

Nothing hurts more than trying to mend back the pieces to a broken heart. Broken from a tragic loss or either broken promises. Sometimes all it takes is for the right person to come along to sweep you off of your feet. Then there's times whereas to some words are better left unsaid. Sure no one is going to love you like the last person loved you. Not even the person you might be currently with love is going to stay the same from day one.

LONG DISTANT RELATIONSHIPS:

In, some instances long distance relationships work for some people. And in other instances you never know how many sex partners your mate has had before you. He or she might tell you what they want you to hear. But some men and women don't know each other well as they think they do. Some men might say to themselves, oh my girl will never cheat on me. And, some women will say I will never give my man a reason not to trust me.

APPROPRIATE CALL HOURS:

Truth be told, there's a certain time to stop calling someone's house. The best call hours should be from 12-10pm unless it's an emergency. An emergency meaning a life or death type of situation. Some people work all sorts of different hours of the day. Either that or they are trying to catch up on some much needed sleep. When some people get less than the recommended amount of sleep they be cranky the day after that.

LOVE SCRATCHES:

Ladies let your man come home with scratches all over his back; you might be bound to go ghetto hood on him. First thing might come to mind is to key his car. Not even that but go to the girl house and drop his clothes off on her front lawn. Some women might leave a note to her man's mistress. The note might say he's your problem now make sure you wash his dirty boxers by the way. And by the way he likes Downy fabric softener on his clothes.

OVERNIGHT HOE BAG:

Let me break it down to you when a female carries an overnight hoe bag and what it consists of. It's when you see a female in a fast food restaurant at about 1:17a.m. On a Sunday morning brushing her teeth with no toothpaste. Inside her purse were a box of latex condoms. And to make matters seems a little awkward she went in the direction of a motel. But, sure as lit wood she didn't go to that motel hungry at all. By ordering a late night meal to fill her up.

WOMEN BEING FORWARD:

First and foremost, there's nothing wrong with a woman being forward under certain circumstances. She sees something or someone she wants so she takes the forward approach. It doesn't make her less of a woman. But, a woman shouldn't do is ask a man to marry her at all. Most men then feel like that takes away a bit of their man hood. That they're being cornered and pressed into marrying a woman. It might take away a bit of their spunk.

STATING THE OBVIOUS:

Whenever a man or woman has to buy their mate's affection then, what type of love is that? It entails that their relationship or marriage is based off buying the other person love. That especially when a man knows that he's in the dog house he'll rush out to buy some expensive jewelry and roses. Though, some women way of apologizing to their man is either dinner or makeup sex. But, if she knows her man is really mad she'll give him some breathing space to calm down. Some women will go far as to staying over a friend's house. Or a man will change their number.

HUSTLE GAME:

There's nothing wrong with a woman trying to get her hustle game on. It shows she's independent and wants to be her own boss someday. She doesn't want to feel like she has to answer to anybody. Like some people are born with silver spoons in their mouth. The thing is that when some men or women get a little ounce of power they seem to overuse their power. Some fail to realize as quick as you got the power you can lose it. Just as in some women have never had to worry about working a day in their lives.

COMMITMENT ISSUES:

Yes some men as well as women have commitment issues. You have some men that are afraid to commit to one woman. And some women feel that they have options so why settle. Some women that do settle feel like they deserve more. It's the fact of the matter that some women are just use to being spoiled. To being able to get their way all the time. As in to say if you can't commit to making a simple dinner then you get frustrated. Some men and women both are tired of the it's me not you speech.

FEMALES CASHING OUT:

Black card, American Express or Capital One some women get their money bags the best way they know how. Sure, there's nothing wrong with a woman being a female escort. A woman in that field just has to stray strapped at all times. Some females stay ready to cash out the first time they catch their man doing wrong. Not only that but a woman should have a secret money stash for a rainy day. Every woman has to have her personals on her at all times.

RESPECT A WOMAN'S PRIVACY:

Almost nothing tears down a woman's self-esteem or pride then for her lover or man to expose nude photos of her. And to leak a sex video that the two of them did together. Her man or ex lover will say you sure you didn't leak the video yourself of us yourself. Or someone took his phone and leaked it that way. Now really what woman is going to leak her own sex video to the public as a publicity stunt? Especially when she's trying to get her career back on track. In some sort of way she might still have feelings for you. Just remember though sometimes a man doesn't know what he's dealing with especially if the woman he's dealing with is a strong-minded person.

SIDE CHIC TRIAL:

Baby hand me your phone so we can link up later is what a man might say to his side piece. I'm going to put my number in your phone call or text me with the directions to the meet up spot is what your average side chic might say. I don't know if we should do this might be the first thought that comes to mind. Do you have a wife, girlfriend or baby mama will be the follow up questions. For real though ladies do your homework before committing to anyone.

MAKEUP SEX:

There's nothing like having a small petty disagreement with your man just to have some makeup sex. Makeup sex just to hear him say who does this belongs to? Then you scream his name out even louder than usual. You might tell him big daddy it's yours. He gives it to you doggy style with your legs in the air. You both have sweat dripping from your bodies. Be sure to grab hold of the sheets it's about to be a bumpy ride.

FEELINGS OF EMPTINESS INSIDE:

True love comes around once maybe twice in a lifetime. Grab hold of your true feelings and try not to confuse the difference between love and sex. Some people say that they can get sex any day of the week. But, true love is something that's very rare. Both female and males say oh he or she say they love me but they're making plans with someone else. You're placed on the back burner. The last priority of the day or you just won't even get a text for a rain check. Think to yourself, do you really know your worth? Don't go to tripping inside. Mentally you will be okay as time goes on.

DON'T COME FOR ME:

Don't come for me unless you're ready for what's at the end of my fist. Respect me and mines because you don't want these problems. Man it's crazy what some females would do once you invade their personal space. But, the first sign of disrespect towards some females you never know what you're about to be up against. A person size might fool you at times. They could be someone who has never fought a day in their lives. Rest assured you never know what a person is hiding under their bed. So be cautious and don't jump stupid. Be wise.

INSIDE THE WORLD OF CELEBACY:

You entice your man with the start of sex pulling your man towards you, but he pulls back. You ask him is it something I said or did. He replies with a no then you think to yourself is there another woman? Don't sale yourself short when your man has been away from you for a while. Your man has been in army combat for months and you know he got to be faithful. You were the first person to cross his mind so he surprised you and showed up to your front door. After he tells you that he's celibant you decide to then join him and his celibacy journey.

RIDE OR DIE TYPE OF CHIC:

In life some men just don't realize how good they have it when it comes down to their relationship. Some men have that ride or die type of chic. A chic that will do whatever for you because she loves you. If you need her to go cuss out one of your enemies she'll do it for you. If you need her to go bust a window or two out she's down for whatever. In some instances a woman won't take a bullet for you. But, what she will do is give you a fair warning if someone has a hit out on you.

INFIDELITY RECEIPTS

ACT ONE

Setting: In the living room of Jessica's apartment

At Rise: Jessica and her best friend Lauren have a discussion about their dating lives and therapy on her couch

JESSICA
Lauren, what are you and your boo doing for your anniversary next week?

LAUREN
Might be in the midst of going our separate ways. He's been acting strange as of lately.

JESSICA
Have you ever thought about going to therapy? It can maybe give you some sort of hope.
(Lauren nods her head)

LAUREN
What makes you think that I want some therapist all up in my business judging me?

JESSICA
She's a good therapist and she doesn't pass judgment on you.

LAUREN
How do you know she won't pass judgment on me?
(Jessica nods her head)

JESSICA
She's been where you are before about eight years ago.

LAUREN
Is this before or after she became a therapist?

JESSICA
Now, look who's quick to pass judgment on someone.

LAUREN
It's nothing like that. I'm just tired of having my feelings toyed with and I'm on my last straw.

JESSICA
When did you decide that you were on your last straw? Before or after your man mistress took to the blogs.

LAUREN
Some shady friend you are.

JESSICA
If I don't call you out on your shade then, what type of friend will I be?

LAUREN
The type who needs to mind her own business and knows when I want her input I will ask for it.

Lauren phone rings and it's a text message from her boyfriend Luke
Jessica slides over to read Lauren's text out loud

(Didn't I ask you to not have your ex calling my house and I'm the one pays all the bills and supports us.)

JESSICA
Last time I checked, I thought you only had one daddy.

LAUREN
Can't a woman just have her privacy sometimes?

JESSICA
At least my man isn't confused about his sexuality.

LAUREN
Let's go to your man's job and see if he's working right now.

JESSICA
Let's do that then. I want to surprise my boo with some lunch today.

Jessica and Lauren leave her apartment to go surprise Lawrence her boyfriend.
Jessica and Lauren arrive at the massage parlor

LAWERENCE
Jess what are you and your boogie friend doing here? It would've been nice if you would've call first.

JESSICA
All you ever have is one client every hour and I thought you might could use some lunch.

LAWERENCE
As a matter of a fact I have a client on the way in like five minutes.

JESSICA
All you ever do is have female clients, why you never have any male clients?

LAWERENCE
Woman, I'm 100% all man and only massage women.

Lauren interrupts Lawerence

LAUREN
So what are you trying to say? Men don't massage men unless they're sick or on the DL.

LAWERENCE
Sorry if I might have offended you in some sort of way but, I meant nothing by it.

LAUREN
None taken. I've had enough of almost everyone throwing jabs at my man. Is there something I need to know?

LAWERENCE
If he hasn't told you himself then it's not my place to say anything.

LAUREN
Because you're a man are you trying to say that you don't want to be the one to gossip like a female?

LAWERENCE
My point exactly, it's mostly a female thing.

Jessica nods her head.

JESSICA
Lauren girl let's go we've already over stayed our welcome.

LAUREN
I've been thrown out of better places. Between you and your man I'm going to really need to see that therapist now.

JESSICA
What day and time would you like for me to set up the appointment for?

LAUREN
I'm a grown woman, I know how to dial seven digits myself.

Lawerence walks Jessica and Lauren to the door.

Lauren and Luke meet up at the therapist office

LADY T
What brings you two here to my office today?

LAUREN
The streets and a few of my friends are saying my man is on the DL that they have receipts.

LUKE
(Turns to the therapist)
Doc, if she wanted to know that all she had to do was ask me and I would've told her.

LADY T
By you being a man you only should be with who makes you happy.

LAUREN
I'm not making you happy like I thought I was.

LUKE
It's not that you're not making me happy. I just don't feel free to be myself around you.

LADY T
At least we're making some sort of progress here.

CURTAINS CLOSE

INSPIRATIONS IN MY LIFE

Not many people have been an inspiration in my life thus far. Because I don't have very many people that I associate myself with. I have really one loyal female friend that I associate with outside of work. Her name is Paula P. And my God-mother has been an inspiration to me since I was a teenager. Even more so my best friend and former boyfriend of eleven years was also my inspiration. He would say to ask questions that you don't know the answer to.

PREVIOUS BOOKS PUBLISHED

1. Together as a couple we have the guidelines
2. The Pros & Cons of Knowing a woman
3. Memorable Moments
4. Celebrity Crushes
5. My Lost Love
6. Reasons to Mind your meds

ABOUT THE AUTHOR

As an author, I write some of my best writings observing certain situations. Trying to stay far away from stress and migraine related situations doesn't always work. There's stress in working some days. And there's migraine headaches when I don't have the appetite to eat anything. Though, the thing is to not let no more than four hours go by or I might have that nausea feeling. It's just that I miss my best friend Ronald Mobley and my world hasn't been the same since he passed last November of 2017.

Printed by Libri Plureos GmbH in Hamburg, Germany